My State
WISCONSIN

By Christina Earley

TABLE OF CONTENTS

Wisconsin 3

Glossary 22

Index 24

A Crabtree Seedlings Book

Crabtree Publishing
crabtreebooks.com

School-to-Home Support for Caregivers and Teachers

This book helps children grow by letting them practice reading. Here are a few guiding questions to help the reader build his or her comprehension skills. Possible answers appear in red.

Before Reading:

• What do I know about Wisconsin?
  - *I know that Wisconsin is a state.*
  - *I know that Wisconsin is famous for its cheese.*

• What do I want to learn about Wisconsin?
  - *I want to learn which famous people were born in Wisconsin.*
  - *I want to learn what the state flag looks like.*

During Reading:

• What have I learned so far?
  - *I have learned that Madison is the state capital of Wisconsin.*
  - *I have learned that Apostle Islands National Lakeshore consists of 21 islands.*

• I wonder why...
  - *I wonder why the state flower is the common blue violet.*
  - *I wonder why Sheboygan is known for its bratwurst.*

After Reading:

• What did I learn about Wisconsin?
  - *I have learned that Schoolhouse Beach has rocks instead of sand.*
  - *I have learned that the state animal is the American badger.*

• Read the book again and look for the glossary words.
  - *I see the word **shore** on page 4, and the word **capital** on page 6. The other glossary words are found on pages 22 and 23.*

I live in Sheboygan. It is along the **shore** of Lake Michigan.

My city is known for its **bratwurst**.

Wisconsin is in the **midwestern** United States. The **capital** is Madison.

Fun Fact: Milwaukee is the largest city in Wisconsin.

The state animal is the American badger.

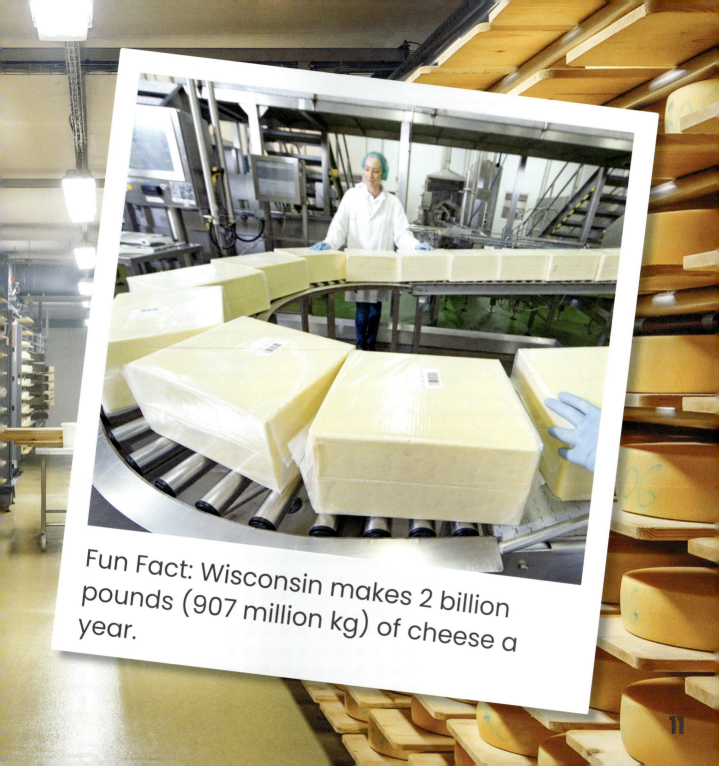

Fun Fact: Wisconsin makes 2 billion pounds (907 million kg) of cheese a year.

My state flag is blue. The state **coat of arms** is in the middle.

There are three national sports teams in Wisconsin.

I like to visit the Apostle Islands National Lakeshore in winter. The ice caves are my favorite.

Fun Fact: The Apostle Islands National Lakeshore consists of 21 islands.

I like to explore Cave of the Mounds. The total length of the cave is 1,692 feet (516 m).

Actor Mark Ruffalo was born in Wisconsin. Racecar driver Danica Patrick was also born in Wisconsin.

Fun Fact: Arthur Davidson and William S. Harley, **cofounders** of the Harley-Davidson motorcycle company, were born in Milwaukee, Wisconsin.

Schoolhouse Beach is one of the few beaches in the world that has rocks instead of sand!

Glossary

bratwurst (brat-werst): A type of sausage, usually made of pork

capital (cap-ih-tuhl): The city or town where the government of a country, state, or province is located

coat of arms (coht uv armz): A special group of pictures, usually shown on a shield

cofounder (koh-foun-der): A person who starts a business with other people

midwestern (mid-west-urn): The northern central part of the United States

shore (shor): The land along the edge of a body of water

Index

badger 8
cheese 10, 11
ice caves 14
Ruffalo, Mark 18
Schoolhouse Beach 20
Sheboygan 4, 5

About the Author

Christina Earley lives in sunny South Florida with her husband and son. She enjoys traveling around the United States and learning about different historical places. Her hobbies include hiking, yoga, and baking.

Written by: Christina Earley
Designed and Illustrated by: Bobbie Houser
Series Development: James Earley
Proofreader: Melissa Boyce
Educational Consultant: Marie Lemke M.Ed.

Photographs:
Alamy: INTERFOTO/History: p. 19, 23
Shutterstock: MarynaG: cover; Checubus: p. 3; Jacob Boomsma: p. 4, 23; Rick Kessinger: p. 5, 22; Volina: p. 6, 22-23; Sean Pavone: p. 7; Jim Cumming: p. 8; Predrag Lukic: p. 9; Sergey_Bogomyako: p. 10-11; Juice Flair: p. 11; railway fx: p. 12, 22; Mark Herreid: p. 13; Gottography: p. 14; critterbiz: p. 14-15; Sarah Michals: p. 16; Aaron of L.A. Photography: p. 17; Tinseltown: p. 18 left; Grindstone Media Group: p. 18 right; Retired Guy Photography: p. 20; Oleksandr Koretskyi: p. 21

Crabtree Publishing

crabtreebooks.com   800-387-7650
Copyright © 2024 Crabtree Publishing
All rights reserved. No part of this publication may be reproduced, stored in a retrieval system or be transmitted in any form or by any means, electronic, mechanical, photocopying, recording, or otherwise, without the prior written permission of Crabtree Publishing.

Printed in the U.S.A./072023/CG20230214

Published in Canada
Crabtree Publishing
616 Welland Avenue
St. Catharines, Ontario
L2M 5V6

Published in the United States
Crabtree Publishing
347 Fifth Avenue
Suite 1402-145
New York, New York, 10016

Library and Archives Canada Cataloguing in Publication
Available at Library and Archives Canada

Library of Congress Cataloging-in-Publication Data
Available at the Library of Congress

Hardcover: 978-1-0398-0543-9
Paperback: 978-1-0398-0575-0
Ebook (pdf): 978-1-0398-0639-9
Epub: 978-1-0398-0607-8